THE LITTLE BOOK OF
CAKE
DECORATING
TIPS

AVENT

THE LITTLE BOOK OF
CAKE
DECORATING
TIPS

MEG AVENT

Absolute Press

First published in Great Britain in 2008 by
Absolute Press
Scarborough House, 29 James Street West
Bath BA1 2BT, England
Phone 44 (0) 1225 316013 **Fax** 44 (0) 1225 445836
E-mail info@absolutepress.co.uk
Web www.absolutepress.co.uk

A catalogue record of this book is available
from the British Library

ISBN 13: 9781904573968

Printed and bound in China by 1010

'All the world is birthday cake, so take a piece, but not too much.'

George Harrison

When **mixing coloured icing, make more than you need,** as it may be difficult to achieve exactly the same colour again.

2

To **prevent crimping tools springing open** and tearing your sugar paste, tie an elastic band around them.

A quick and easy way to decorate a sponge cake is to place a paper doily on top of the cake and shake icing sugar over it – take away the doily and you have an impressive pattern!

4

Always **keep a separate wooden spoon** especially **for beating royal icing.** General-use spoons could be greasy and grease prevents egg whites expanding properly.

5

One way to **make your own embosser** is by placing your design under a piece of Perspex or glass, and, using a fine tube, **pipe** royal icing **around the outline of the drawing.**

Once dry, lift the outline off the glass and press the design onto soft sugar paste.

6

Never try and get away with using **soft margarine** to make buttercream; it won't taste good and will be **too soft for piping.**

7

It's not always easy to cut a cake perfectly level just with an ordinary knife. To make it easier

invest in a cake leveller

and just set it to the desired height.

To make professional looking sugar flowers,

roll the flower paste very thinly

– so thin in fact, you could almost read through it.

If your knife is sticking to the buttercream whilst icing, don't panic, just **dip it occasionally into hot water,** dry, and then continue to use.

10

If you feel **daunted by the thought of writing freehand** straight onto a cake, use either an embosser, or special cutters or moulds to form letters out of sugar paste.

While working with royal icing,

remember that sugar dries extremely quickly, so always place a piece of dampened clingfilm or muslin over the bowl to prevent it drying out.

12

To **prevent the buttercream** in a piping bag **getting too warm** from your hands on a hot day – use a double thickness bag.

13

When making marzipan and sugar **paste models** for children's novelty cakes, **use raw dried spaghetti** instead of cocktail sticks to support their heads and limbs.

14

Before slicing a cake into layers,

make sure they can be replaced in their correct positions by cutting a small 'V' shape down the side of the cake. Use this 'V' as a guide when replacing the layers.

15

To use **ganache for piping,** first refrigerate, and when firm, beat to a piping consistency.

16

Before placing a cake in a box,

put a folded cloth or non-slip mat onto the base of the box. This will raise the cake slightly and make it easier to grip the cake board when lifting the cake from the box later.

17

Sugar paste does not like to get wet – moisture will dissolve the sugar leaving craters, so

keep all utensils clean and thoroughly dry.

18

For a **glossier ganache, use double or whipping cream** rather than single; they both have a higher fat content which helps create the gloss.

19

For creamier chocolaty buttercream with a lovely intense colour and taste, don't add the cocoa powder straight to the butter, instead, **dissolve it first in a little hot water** to form a paste and then add.

20

Condensation can form on a chocolate cake taken straight from the freezer.
To avoid this happening,

move the cake to the fridge to defrost the day before it's needed.

21

Paste food colours are better for colouring sugar pastes as opposed to liquid colours that can make the icing too sticky. But be warned, they **are** surprisingly **vibrant, so add very gradually** using a cocktail stick.

22

Having trouble piping?

Try brushing away mistakes

with a damp paintbrush and try again.

23

If you would like an impressive looking 3-tier cake for a wedding, but two tiers will be sufficient cake for your guests,

consider using a dummy tier

for the third. They are widely available from cake decorating suppliers and can be decorated in just the same way as the other tiers. Just remember to tell the caterers!

24

Always use a metal ruler

(known as a straight edge) to level the top of a royal iced cake; a plastic one will bend under the weight of the icing and leave ridges.

25

Use **two thin coats of buttercream,** rather than one thick one, to achieve a **truly smooth and even icing.**

26

To prevent getting into **a sticky mess when making marzipan roses;**

place the petals between two sheets of polythene and thin the petals through the surface.

27

To make sugar roses look more real, always make the centres a slightly deeper colour than the outside petals.

28

Before you pour icing

over your fondant fancies,

place a sheet of greaseproof

paper under the rack.

Any fondant that drips onto the paper below can be scraped off and reused.

29

For complete accuracy, **always measure for a template after the cake has been iced** – not before. If taken directly from the cake surface the template will be too small.

30

To **prevent sugar paste frills becoming floppy** while drying, place a thin layer of scrunched cling film under the frill until it has dried. Just remember to remove it!

31

To prevent any loose crumbs from sticking to your icing or marzipan – coat the cake with either jam or buttercream first.

32

Brush marzipan animals and fruits with

confectioner's glaze to give them

a lovely shine.

Be sure to clean your brush with glaze cleaner afterwards.

33

When **rolling out sugar paste** or marzipan to cover a cake, **use a pair of** specially designed **spacers** to ensure it is rolled to an equal thickness.

34

Worry no more! When taking a special event cake to a venue,

pack a 'first aid kit'

of filled piping bag and sugar flowers, in case of emergency repairs.

35

When working with dark coloured sugar paste, lightly grease the work surface with white vegetable fat instead of icing sugar to prevent sticking. If you use icing sugar, white flecks could appear on the dark surface and will be almost impossible to remove.

36

Madeira cake is the most suitable for **cutting into different shapes** as it is less likely to crumble. Or, if using a different type of sponge, **freeze and cut** into shape while it is still semi-frozen.

37

If your cake isn't as uniform as you would like,

use buttercream to fill any holes or cracks

and place the cake in the fridge for a couple of hours to set before icing.

38

If you are daunted by the thought of painting directly onto a cake surface, **try painting your design onto a sugar paste plaque** instead, that way if you go wrong you can always start again. Plaques can also be made well ahead of time.

39

To **prevent your hand wobbling** when piping onto a cake, support the icing bag with the fingers of your opposite hand and **keep your elbow close** to your body.

40

When attempting to pipe a straight line, always

pipe towards yourself, not away.

41

When royal icing appears too soft, always try beating it first

before attempting to thicken it with more sugar. The beating alone may well stiffen it sufficiently, but adding too much sugar could make it too heavy.

42

To achieve a soft sheen on your sugar paste icing, **gently polish** it with the palm of your hand, or better still, a special cake smoother.

43

A simple way to decorate a cake

covered with buttercream is to sieve a light coating of cocoa powder over the surface, and then, using the blade of a knife, draw across the cake in lines to form a feather effect.

44

Just before icing a cake already covered with **marzipan, brush the surface with a little clear alcohol,** such as gin or vodka, **to prevent any bacteria** forming between the layers.

45

If **cracks** have appeared in your sugar paste icing and it is still soft, rub gently with your hand, or, if need be, wait a day to let it dry and **fill with a small amount of paste** softened with water.

46

Left-handed decorators do not despair

– some suppliers sell petal tubes especially for left-handed people.

47

When making sugar paste models, **use a cutting wheel** to shape the paste instead of a knife as **it won't drag** and distort the paste.

48

Always **use chocolate plastique** rather than ganache to cover a multi-tiered cake as it is **more stable.**

49

To make tiny chocolate curls the easy way, **use a potato peeler** to shave the curls off the side of a block of chocolate.

50

To colour white chocolate, use powdered food colouring.

Liquid colouring will cause the chocolate to thicken and become unusable.

Meg Avent

Meg Avent specialises in creating bespoke wedding and celebration cakes. After gaining experience working with one of London's top cake decorators, she now runs her own business, Lemon Sky Cakes.

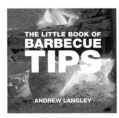

THE LITTLE BOOK OF
**BARBECUE
TIPS**

ANDREW LANGLEY

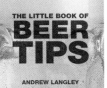

THE LITTLE BOOK OF
**BEER
TIPS**

ANDREW LANGLEY

THE LITTLE BOOK OF
**HERB
TIPS**

WILLIAM FORTT

THE LITTLE BOOK OF
**POKER
TIPS**

PETER FRENCH

THE LITTLE BOOK OF
**GARDENING
TIPS**

WILLIAM FORTT

THE LITTLE BOOK OF
CHEFS' TIPS

RICHARD MAGGS

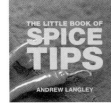

THE LITTLE BOOK OF
**SPICE
TIPS**

ANDREW LANGLEY

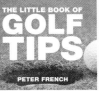

THE LITTLE BOOK OF
**GOLF
TIPS**

PETER FRENCH

THE LITTLE BOOK OF
**TIPS
SERIES**

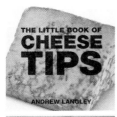

THE LITTLE BOOK OF
CHEESE
TIPS

ANDREW LANGLEY

THE LITTLE BOOK OF
WINE
TIPS

ANDREW LANGLEY

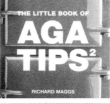

THE LITTLE BOOK OF
AGA
TIPS²

RICHARD MAGGS

THE LITTLE BOOK OF
COFFEE
TIPS

ANDREW LANGLEY

THE LITTLE BOOK OF
TEA
TIPS

ANDREW LANGLEY

THE LITTLE BOOK OF
AGA
TIPS³

RICHARD MAGGS

THE LITTLE BOOK OF
AGA
TIPS

RICHARD MAGGS

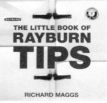

THE LITTLE BOOK OF
CHRISTMAS
AGA
TIPS

RICHARD MAGGS

THE LITTLE BOOK OF
RAYBURN
TIPS

RICHARD MAGGS

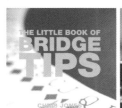

THE LITTLE BOOK OF
BRIDGE
TIPS

CHRIS JONES

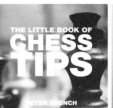

THE LITTLE BOOK OF
CHESS
TIPS

PETER ARENCH

THE LITTLE BOOK OF
FISHING
TIPS

MICK DEVENISH

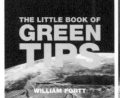

THE LITTLE BOOK OF
GREEN
TIPS

WILLIAM FORTT

THE LITTLE BOOK OF
KITTEN
TIPS

ANDREW LANGLEY

THE LITTLE BOOK OF
MARMITE
TIPS

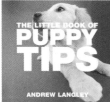

THE LITTLE BOOK OF
PUPPY
TIPS

ANDREW LANGLEY

THE LITTLE BOOK OF
WHISKY
TIPS

ANDREW LANGLEY

THE LITTLE BOOK OF
TRAVEL
TIPS

MEGAN DEVENISH

Little Books of Tips from Absolute Press

Aga Tips
Aga Tips 2
Aga Tips 3
Backgammon Tips
Barbecue Tips
Beer Tips
Bread Tips
Bridge Tips
Cake Decorating Tips
Cheese Tips
Chefs' Tips
Chess Tips
Christmas Aga Tips
Coffee Tips
Fishing Tips
Gardening Tips
Golf Tips
Green Tips

Hair Tips
Herb Tips
Houseplant Tips
Kitten Tips
Marmite Tips
Nail Tips
Olive Oil Tips
Poker Tips
Puppy Tips
Rayburn Tips
Scrabble Tips
Spice Tips
Tea Tips
Travel Tips
Vinegar Tips
Whisky Tips
Wine Tips

**All titles: £2.99 /
112 pages**